TIKTOK MARKETING STRATEGY

The Definitive Guide to TikTok Marketing Tactics for Businesses

BY

Ejeke P.C

BONUS

This is My Way of Saying Thank You. You'll Also Get These Fast Action Bonuses...

Fast Action Bonus #1 – TikTok Marketing - Cheat Sheet (Valued at $27)

This cheat sheet is a handy checklist that makes it easy to get started.

It breaks up the entire guide into easy-to-follow steps so that you can make sure you have all the highlights of everything covered inside right at your fingertips.

Fast Action Bonus #2 – TikTok Marketing - Mind Map (Valued at $17)

Some people learn better by looking at a mind map. The mind map gives you an overview of everything covered inside the guide. You can also print it out for quick reference anytime you need it!

Fast Action Bonus #3 – TikTok Marketing - Resource Guide (Valued at $17)

The Resource Guide gives you a quick point of reference to all of the resources mentioned throughout the guide.

This is my way of saying thank to you for buying this book. To get the bonus, **scan the QR-Code below** to download the pdf and enjoy!

PLEASE WRITE A REVIEW!

If this book helped you out in anyway, please help me to help others by writing a review!

CLICK HERE TO LEAVE A REVIEW

Still, if you did not get anything new from this book or you were not impacted in some way, I would still like to hear what you have to say. Either way, I will know what am doing right or wrong and to improve in the future. I wouldn't like to take your money and not deliver. So please, take just 2 minutes to let me know what you think.

Everyone is searching for help on how to improve their lives for the better and one thing they do look for are reviews. If this book has a lot amazing reviews with great comments, they will buy the book and read it and so the ripples effects of goodness spreads. But if it doesn't have any great reviews and comments, they don't buy the book and read it.

I know this book can positively impact and help someone and you can help that person by writing your thoughts and takeaways from the book.

Additionally, I would like to read your review and hear how this book has helped you in anyway at shape or form. My plan is to print every single review and hang them on my home office wall to read for inspiration and motivation throughout the day.

Your great review helps me personally to stay focused and be able to validate all the hard work and lots of hours invested in preparing this book for you.

CLICK THE LINK TO LEAVE A REVIEW

Thank you again for reading this book and all of your support, I am truly honoured and grateful to have been of help. I look forward to helping you make this year the best ever for you and your family!

LEGAL DISCLAIMER:

Any earnings or income statements, or earnings or income examples, are only estimates of what we think you could earn. There is no assurance you'll do as well. If you rely upon our figures, you must accept the risk of not doing as well. Where specific income figures are used, and attributed to an individual or business, those persons or businesses have earned that amount. There is no assurance you'll do as well. If you rely upon our figures; you must accept the risk of not doing as well.

Any and all claims or representations, as to income earnings on this web site, are not to be considered as average earnings. There can be no assurance that any prior successes, or past results, as to income earnings, can be used as an indication of your future success or results.

Monetary and income results are based on many factors. We have no way of knowing how well you will do, as we do not know you, your background, your work ethic, or your business skills or practices. Therefore, we do not guarantee or imply that you will win any incentives or prizes that may be offered, get rich, that you will do as well, or make any money at all. There is no assurance you'll do as well. If you rely upon our figures; you must accept the risk of not doing as well.

Internet businesses and earnings derived there from, have

unknown risks involved, and are not suitable for everyone. Making decisions based on any information presented in our products, services, or web site, should be done only with the knowledge that you could experience significant losses, or make no money at all.

All products and services by our company are for educational and informational purposes only. Use caution and seek the advice of qualified professionals. Check with your accountant, lawyer or professional advisor, before acting on this or any information.

Users of our products, services and web site are advised to do their own due diligence when it comes to making business decisions and all information, products, and services that have been provided should be independently verified by your own qualified professionals. Our information, products, and services on this web site should be carefully considered and evaluated, before reaching a business decision, on whether to rely on them. All disclosures and disclaimers made herein or on our site, apply equally to any offers, prizes, or incentives, that may be made by our company.

You agree that our company is not responsible for the success or failure of your business decisions relating to any information presented by our company, or our company products or services.

INTRODUCTION

Unless you have been living under a rock, you probably must have heard about TikTok. Just like most social media platforms exploded on to the scene, Tiktok was no exception. Its explosive growth has been phenomenal to least the lest. It grown from a little-known app that was lunched in China to be a global force. A force so huge that even politicians cannot ignore it.

Why you may ask? And why not, the world is going through one of its roughest patches yet. From Climate change to know the Covid-19 Pandemic. Lots of people are fed-up with the circle of negative news that people are looking some release.

Fortunately, Tiktok has come to fill that role. Yes, there were other social platforms but Tiktok is new, fresh and different. So, again why not? Tiktok has grown to over 500 million users and counting. These are users who are looking for some fun, Excitement and release, and the platform provides that pure and simple.

We all know that where there are lots of people, there will be massive opportunities. The question now is:

1- **Are you ready to put the platform to your advantage?**
2- **And just how exactly are you going to do that?**
3- **Do you have what it takes to succeed on the platform?**
4- **Is the platform suited to your kind of business**?

These questions and many more will be answered in this little book. So, please read on.

For you as a business owner or as a business entity to be successful with TikTok marketing, you must study the platform and do all the research that needs to be done to more than the average guy. You need to know not just how the platform works but also what it stands for. And also, like all platforms, what kind of demographic does it attract?

The latter is easy, all you need to know is to get on the platform and by the time you have scrolled a couple of pages then you will kind of a get a feel as to the age group that the platform most appeals to. That is the younger generation.

The younger generation also have their own language and you need to get with the times if you are going to be successful.

With this book in your hands, I made you that you get all the information and know how on the best route to follow when making your marketing plans so you will have the best chance of success.

No doubt, this book is an easy read. Everything is explained simply and to the point. This book is quite the opposite of all the TikTok book you will on this subject. So, go ahead dig in; but what's most important is your ability to implement what you read.

In this book, you are not only going to learn the intricacies of marketing on Tiktok but you will also get to see real world business that applied all the strategies mentioned in this book and the successes that you stand to gain.

Something else that you already know which needs repeating is that with any kind of social media platform, engagement is key. And I mean constant and sustained engagement is very important. And you will get all these in this book.

A lot of businesses have tried marketing with tiktok and to fail. There is a reason for anything that happens whether you intended it or not. So, make your intentions clear right from the beginning and act accordingly.

Be sure of your objectives from the start and have a realistic projection of your end point that way you can analyse your progress. I also talked about this quite a bit in this book. So, you read on and be ready to profit.

Tiktok-What Exactly is it and Why Should Businesses like yours Pay Attention?

Believe it or not, there is quite a good number of CEOs that have never head of Tiktok. That is not surprising if your business is focused on the older demographic. So, it safe to say that the potential of the platform is lost on so many people and businesses included.

As bad as that may sound my friend, this is a huge opportunity if you get my drift. Where there is less competition there is massive opportunity as I mentioned earlier.

If you remember in the introduction, I talked about just how hugely influential Tiktok has become. Yes, it has gotten quite a bit of press and depending on who you ask, it could be a good thing or it could be a bad thing.

But for what it's worth, a good number of parents are growing increasingly concerned that the platform is having a really negative influence on the minds of their kids and really stunting their social skills.

Not to mention that, there will be a lot of bad actors that are attracted to the popularity of the platform and so some disturbing contents are bound to make their way into the platform. And as you might imagine most parents and authorities are worried about the young ones on the platform.

For example, the platform was banned in India in 2019 following allegations of inappropriate content and predatory behaviour a concern. It was banned again in June 2020 alongside a spate of other Chinese-based apps as tensions between China and India heightened.

And it's also being investigated in the United states over National security concerns as I mention above drawing attention from law makers.

So, Tiktok had stepped up to clean up the platform and have since initiated a move aimed at making sure that all content that did not meet their community guide lines are removed. And of course, this will be an ongoing exercise because there will always be someone willing to make life difficult for the rest.

But I see this as a good a thing if the Tiktok is policing the content that people are putting up on the platform that means it will continue to a safe place for you are as a marketer to promote your business.

Though hit with bad press, Tiktok has continued to see impressive growth. In the last 2 years alone, specifically early part of 2018 the platform has been known to be the most downloaded app on the Google play store. And it continued to do well towards the end of the year and placed 3rd most downloaded app in October.

According to stat watchers, in March 2019 there had been over 1 billion installs of TikTok. There were 660 million downloads in 2018 and in the first quarter of 2019 there were 188 million. There are over 500 million active users of TikTok and 26.5 million of these are from the United States.

Here are some other key statistics about TikTok:

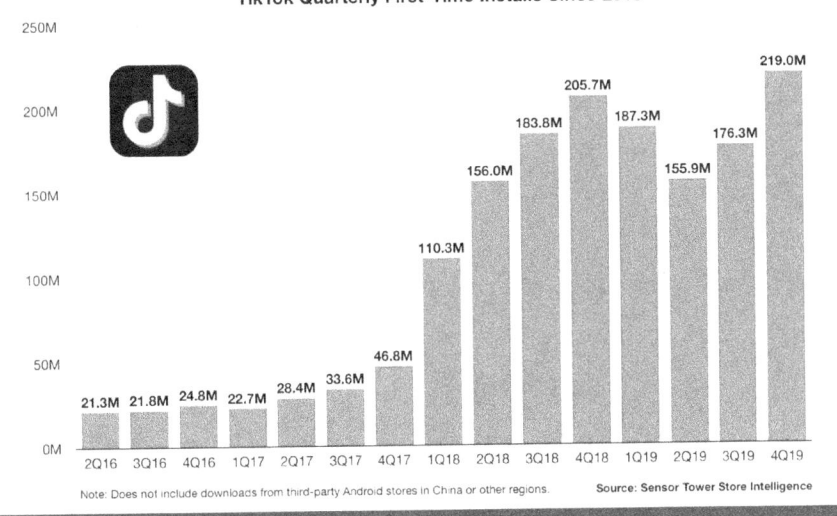

- TikTok MAUs estimated at 800 million

- TikTok downloaded 738 million times in 2019,

- Total TikTok downloads over 1.5 billion – making it the seventh-most downloaded app of the 2010s

- It is estimated that 57% of the TikTok/Douyin userbase is based in China

- India top market for TikTok downloads in 2019 (if we exclude Chinese Android downloads), with 323 million

- 46 million US TikTok downloads in 2019

- Only 9% of US internet users have used TikTok, with 5% more interested in using it; this rises to 49% for teenage users

- ByteDance reports 400 DAU of Douyin in China, and claim 68% of Chinese social media users/59% of smartphone users are Douyin users

- Musical.ly counted 100 million users at time of August 2018 merger with TikTok

- Singer Loren Gray is the most-followed person on TikTok, with close to 40 million followers

- On Douyin, the most-followed account belongs to actor, model, and singer Dilraba Dilmurat, with around 55 million followers

- Android TikTok users spent 68 billion hours using the app in 2019

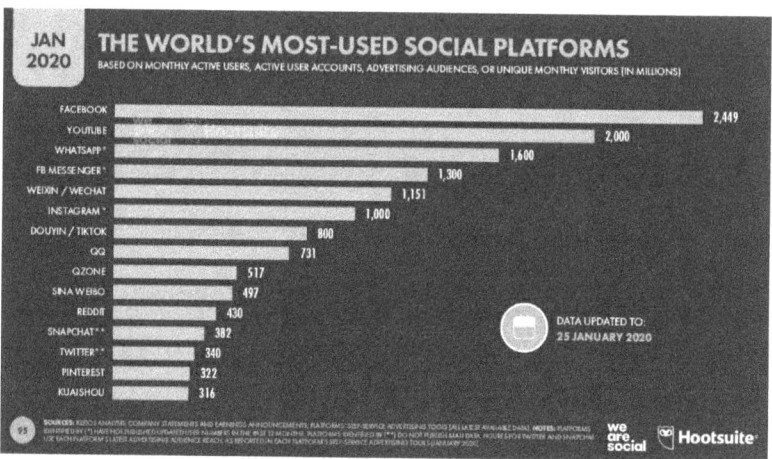

- China accounts for eight out of every 10 minutes viewed on TikTok

- Average daily time on TikTok estimated at 45 minutes

- US users open TikTok an average of eight times a day, with sessions averaging just under 5 minutes

- Indian users spend 38 minutes daily using TikTok

- TikTok one-week retention rate stands at 26%

- A late 2018 Global Web Index study found 55% of TikTok users uploaded a video in the last month, compared to 68% who had watched one

- TikTok 2019 revenue came to $176.9 million (excluding non-iOS Chinese revenue)
- ByteDance controls 23% of the Chinese digital app market
- ByteDance became the world's most highly-valued private start-up, with a valuation of $78 billion after a SoftBank-led $3 billion investment round.

WHAT IS TOK-TOK?

Back in September 2016, a Chinese based company, **ByteDance** developed an app called **Douyin**. This app was developed in record time and was lunched in the Chinese market with just 200 days. Later the following year, they decided to lunch another one aimed at the international market, US to be precise. And they called it TikTok.

TikTok/Douyin parent company ByteDance also owns hugely popular Chinese AI-powered news aggregation platform Toutiao, created by CEO Zhang Yiming at the age of 29 in 2012. Notably, he was not backed by either Alibaba or Tencent. TikTok has succeeded where the latter failed with WeChat – success beyond China.

This was a strategic triumph. In November 2017 ByteDance acquired the popular (also China-based) would-be rival app Musical.ly app for a reported $1 billion. TikTok was merged with Musical.ly in August 2018, with app users' accounts migrated to their TikTok accounts. This was seen as a way for the Chinese app to enter the US market – with Musical.ly already boasting a considerable American audience.

The ByteDance company purchased musical.ly which was a popular app created by a start-up in Shanghai, China who also had an office in Santa Monica in the United States. This helped ByteDance to build a larger video community.

Tiktok has caught the attention of the younger folks. With app, you can record and upload about 15 seconds videos. Most if not all the videos on tiktok are short with lip synchronization dancing, comedy skits, and other physical activities. And of course, you don't need me to tell you that the videos with most talent in any social media platform will become a huge influencer.

Most of the videos are usually 15 seconds or less. But it's also possible to upload videos that are around 60 seconds that tell more in-dept story. Most Tiktok users are in the age range of 13 to 24 olds. dancing, comedy skits, and other physical activities for those within this age range.

Like any other social media platform, changes come as the company grows. Recently, Tiktok has made major changes to the kinds of videos that it allows people to upload to the platform. Now, you can find more videos that are not just lip synch videos giving users a treasure trove of different kinds of videos to enjoy.

As you know success attracts and so now on the platform, you can a whole range of different kinds of celebrities like comedians uploading their stand-up clips. There are also a whole generation of prank videos popping up on the platform. There are skate boarders, different ager and groups of dance videos, fashion and beauty videos and many more.

But it's also interesting and I should point out that not all tiktok users create and upload videos on the platform. Just like YouTube and Instagram, a lot of the users are just there to unwind after a hard day's activities.

These are not creators but simply consumers. This is very important because this is the reason why you bought this book. But a bit more about the platform.

Unlike Instagram, users are not required to connect with other users by following them. If you are a user and you just want to find videos to watch, you simply go to the discovery page and type a keyword and search for the video you want. This is also another important fact to note because this concerns you as a business oner.

On the platform, marketers who are looking for an angle or angles to get on the platform have found that some of the users of the platform simply click like on videos and the number of videos liked has been increasing steadily of the past 12 months.

They also found that a lot more people are willing to share tik-tok videos more than ever before. Another important point note as a marketer. Not only that, you can see other videos that a particular user has watched in the past.

WHO ARE THE TIKTOK USERS?

The app has certainly attracted a different demographic in recent months but initially when it was lunched, the target was the Generation Z demographic focusing on females. This does not mean that the target audience cannot expand and will not expand in the future; a point that marketers will do well to note.

Despite having been on the rather recently in the US, Tiktok has the potential to grow in this very lucrative market.

And also, despite the hype surrounding the app, only 9% of US internet users had used the app, as of October 2019, with a further 5% stating an intention to use it. 49% remained unmoved by the app's appeal, with a further 37% reporting that they had never heard of the app.

It's not certain that the two categories are very likely to be strong areas of focus for the app going forward given TikTok's strong demographic tendencies, but certainly there may be some who can be converted to or informed of the app's merits.

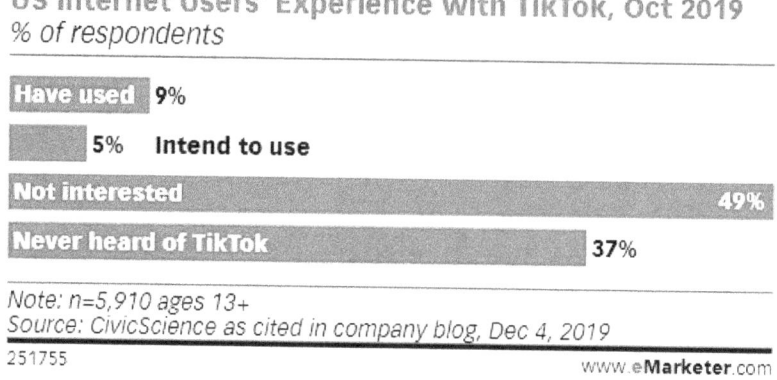

But it's worth noting that 66% of tiktok users are under the 30-year age bracket. And also, that are females are still dominating the platform till date with just about the same percentage.

Think what you will of the platform, it has become a global phenomenon. It has massive international appealed across the globe. And with the adoption rate in Indie and adoption set to explode in the US, the platform will continue to be a force to be reckoned with.

TikTok in Asia

Global Web Index stats show that TikTok penetration is seemingly at its highest in Asia, where over a third of users aged 16-64 had an account. There's not much to split the rest of the world, with penetration of between 12% (North America) and 10% (Latin America and Europe).

TikTok Around the World

% of internet users aged 16-64 who are members of TikTok by global region

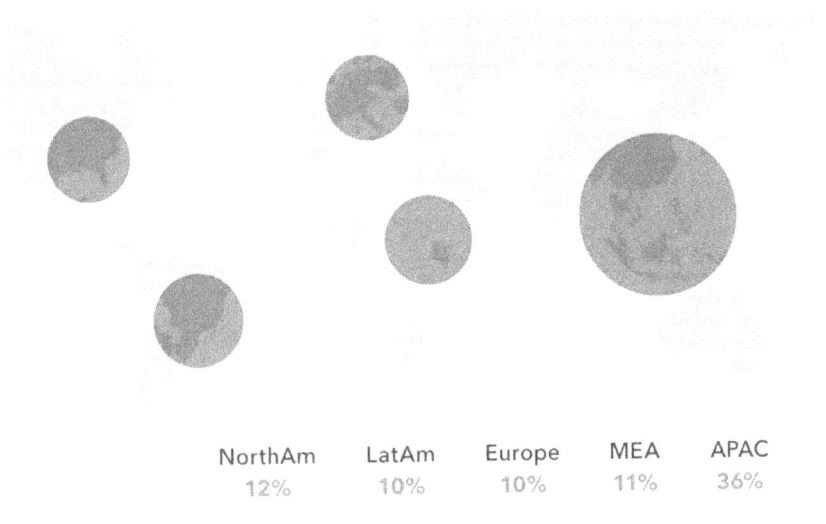

NorthAm	LatAm	Europe	MEA	APAC
12%	10%	10%	11%	36%

As of June 2019, it was estimated that there were 120 million monthly TikTok users in India. But it's not just India where the app is popular.

The Straits Times reported in May 2019 that Southeast Asian downloads of TikTok numbered 190 million. Of these, Indonesia led the way, with 81 million downloads at that point – around 42% of the total.

VIDEOS ON TIKTOK

On the platform, as I mentioned above, you can upload videos easily. The platform has a feature that users can apply to any video to play it at a slow speed or faster. There are also a host of other filters that you can apply.

You can also react to a video someone posted. You can also shoot a video to react to another someone posted earlier on. They also have a popular feature that allows you to place a small window showing the user on the video.

Duet videos have become very popular on the [platform. Here you can create videos that are next to one another and have them play at the same time. This is an adoption form the Musical.ly app after the merger and it was very popular so tiktok decided to keep it. This turns out to be one of the smartest move the app made since it has contributed to the growth of the platform.

On the platform, it's possible for you to upload a video and make them public or private. Or you can also choose to make it that only friends see the video. The application has also adopted the YouTube style of AI application that enables a suggestion of similar videos based on other videos you have watched in the past. This is also good for marketers.

On the platform, each user has the ability to see videos they have saved on their profile and only them can see it unless they decide to share that. On this page, you can add videos, sounds and as well as hashtags and you can refer to them anytime.

Here are some more stats on tiktok-

55% Uploaded a Video in the Last Month

53% of engaged TikTok users claim to have uploaded a video in the last month

54% Commented on a Video

54% of engaged TikTok users claim to have commented on somebody else's video in the last month.

3% Uploaded a "Duet" Video

43% of engaged TikTok users have uploaded a "Duet" video.

63% Liked Someone Else's Video

63% of engaged TikTok users claim to have liked a video in the last month.

68% Watched Someone Else's Videos

68% of engaged TikTok users claim to have watched somebody else's video in the last month.

Behaviors of TikTok Engagers

Behavior	%
Watched someone else's video	68%
Liked someone else's video	63%
Followed someone else	63%
Logged in without doing anything	59%
Uploaded a video	55%
Commented on someone else's video	54%
Shared someone else's video on another social network	50%
Uploaded a "Duet" video	43%
Uploaded a "React" video	41%

TIKTOK GROWTH FACTORS

I have talked quite a bit about the phenomenal growth of Tiktok. A bit more detail here. The platform has earned itself a place on the internet and its growth was quite a surprise for most people in such a short period of time.

But as a marketer, the question is what is behind that growth and is something will hold steady or is it short lived and will feasible out soon?

Let's take a look-

Endorsements from Celebrities-

It's not new that social media has been a really good boon for celebrities. Almost any celebrity has huge following on social platforms. Some more than others but all do have a measure or influence. So, it follows that the more following you have the bigger and far reaching your influence will be.

So, for any celebrity or influencer as will, who has millions of followers, an endorsement from anyone of them will be really huge especially if you are selling something. Think about it, a potentially to reach to millions of people with just a push of the button.

In the talk show circles, one of the biggest celebrities to embraced tiktok was Jimmy Fallon. When he touted one of his challenges on his show and to encourage participate. This help tiktok to add millions of users over night to the platform. Talk about celebrity power.

Though the app has gone international, it still boosts a lot of local content. This is good cos it exposes what happens locally in any country to the rest of the world. On the platform you will see content driven by local folks on the platform from different countries and tiktok is also running a contest that they call "1 Million Audition" across different countries.

In those contests, participants are encouraged to show their talents and make videos with a theme that has best appeal. Any video with the best theme wins the contest. This of course has helped to increase the user base for the app. The platform has also been actively encouraging users by suggesting topics locally depending on where the use is. This has of course led to more locally focused content being uploaded to the platform.

It is easy to use TikTok-
The designers of the platform have made it deliberately easy to for anyone to use the platform. It made sure that the creation and sharing of videos is like a breeze for users. And the growth of the platform is shows this is a smart move as users welcomed it whole heartedly. Just record and upload it's that simple.

When you open the app, you will find that it's very easy to access videos on the platform. Once you start to play a video, the rest will follow sequentially. Because the app is easy to use, it has been noted that 9put of 10 users are on the app multiple times a day.

Three-quarters of all apps are downloaded, accessed once, and then entirely forgotten. With the next TikTok statistic, you can be sure that TikTok falls into the remaining one-quarter.

90 percent of all TikTok users access the app on a daily basis. Not only that, they are extremely active on the app. A study observing the behaviour of TikTok users in the span of one month shows that 68 percent of TikTok users watch someone else's video and 55 percent upload their own videos (Globalwebindex, 2019).

HOW TO START ON TIKTOK

To be successful with tiktok, you need know as much as you can about the platform.

You can be forgiven if you feel like you don't understand TikTok. The app is fast-paced combining elements of Spotify, Snapchat, Vine, and Twitch into a single social network. Here's what you need to know to get started, from TikTok "Challenges" to Coins and Original sounds.

Is TikTok Right for your Business?

Now, just so you know, there is a big question that needs answered before you rush off to get your account on the platform. You need to ask yourself, is this platform suited for my kind business or my target audience and demographic?

That means you have some research and digging to do. So, in addition to the question posed above; to get you started here are some more questions that you need answers to:

- Are your target customers younger than 35 years old?
- Does your business target Generation Z and younger Millennials?
- Are your products visually appealing?
- Are you in the music business or an artist?
- Would you say that your brand is fun, casual and trendy?
- Does your brand have a "cool kid" vibe about it?
- Do you have the resources to post content regularly on TikTok?

This is by no means an exhaustive list. Of course, before you commit any huge chunk of cash to marketing on tiktok, it will pay you to run some initial test with a small amount of money to see how users receive you messaging. That is assuming you have the copy right for the type of demographic that is on the platform.

Install TikTok

The first thing you'll need is a pair of headphones. There's just no way to enjoy TikTok with the sound off. After you download the app, you can immediately start browsing videos. But in order to post any yourself, you'll need to sign up for an account.

TikTok is available for Android and iOS devices here:

Android

iOS

Tiktok has made it really easy to share videos that others have created and as well as your own video. This is not just within the app itself, but you can share these videos on other platy forms and sites as well. This is but yet another reason for you to consider marketing on the platform.

On the platform, as a user, you can actually download full length videos and as well as GIF versions of any content that you upload on the platform. Be aware that there is a watermark on this. But this is a good thing since it helps to get the word out about the platform and you brand very easily. Talk about killing 2 birds with one stone eh!

You can make an account using your email, your phone number, or a third-party platform like Facebook. The app automatically assigns you a username. If you sign up for TikTok with your phone number, the app will generate a generic username such as user1234567. Using an email address generates a more personalized ID (although that may present a privacy issue for users).

To change your username, tap the icon in the right bottom corner that looks like a person's upper body. Then hit Edit Profile. Here, you can change it to something more unique, as well as add a bio, picture, and Profile Video.

By default, TikTok accounts are public, meaning anyone can see your profile and view the videos you post. To adjust these privacy settings, tap the three dots in the top right corner of your profile.

With an email, tiktok will give you a personalised Username. This is not a problem though since you can change this as stated above.

The moment your account is ready and you on the platform, you'll instantly be brought to the feed of videos. I'll show you how it works in step three. But first, tap the icon in the lower right that looks like a person's outline to see and edit your profile.

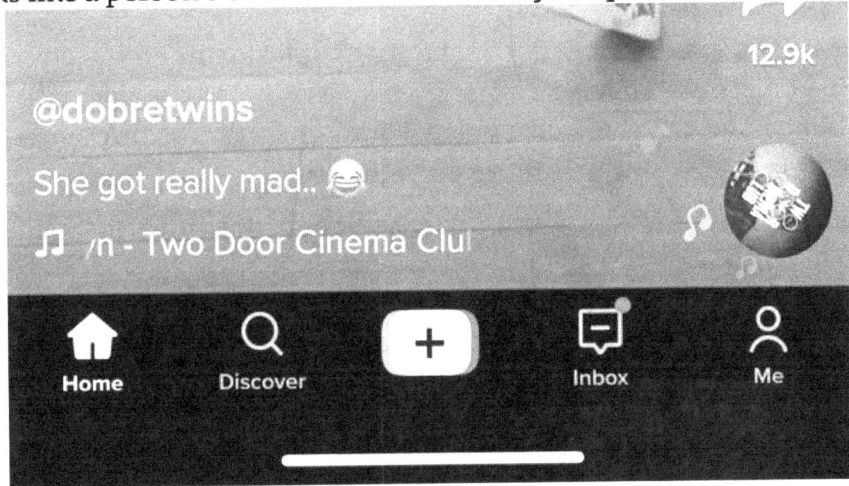

Set up your Profile

Once you enter your profile, tap the Edit Profile button, then select a profile photo or video. You should also add your username and bio information (make sure that this is compelling and appealing to your prospective target audience).

If you want to show off your other social media profiles, you can link up your YouTube and Instagram pages. This very important to help you with brand exposure and as you cross promote your content across platforms. If you're a business, this could be a helpful way to advertise your other visual platforms.

At the time of writing you cannot link your Facebook page at the moment but hopefully this will change in the near future.

Your description very important at this point. You need to take your time to write a very good description and add as much keywords and hashtags that are relevant to your business and your target audience as you can naturally (will talk about this some later).

Also, when you use the duet feature on the app, you will be setting yourself for a lot more engagement with your videos. This you can also set while editing your profile.

Of course, like every social media platform, you need to upload a profile image on your Display section of the app. But with tiktok, you can also add a video. For marketers I recommend using a video. This is much more engaging than a static image. Preferable a short video showcasing your brand will be most ideal.

Always keep n that as you go about setting your account and editing your profile, you have to be thinking in terms of what's best for you target audience, what resonates with them and what they might be willing to engage with.

Start Engaging with other Users

So, after you are inside the app, you need to start engaging with the rest of tiktok users. Find videos that you like start engaging. This is very important cos it will put your brand in the hearts and minds of users on the platform. That is if you did a good a job with videos.

As you use the platform, you will start to get used to it and you will start to see the pattern in users and what kind of content that users like to engage with as the times passes.

Now that you've set up your profile, tap back to the first tab which shows you the video feed.

Think of this feed like Twitter's, but where video is the primary content. If you don't have any followers yet, the app will send you random trending videos. As you begin following and interacting with more people, your feed will become more personalized to your interests.

Now when you find a video that you like, you can find details of the video creator on the right. There will find icons that helps you navigate the different pages or sections of the app. Th 1st icon takes you to content creators page or profile. The next is the heart icon, with this you can "like" the video.

There is also the comments icon for your comments and reactions about the video. The arrow pointing to the right will help you share the "titoks" on other platforms.

The last icon is a spinning record icon with musical notes coming out of it. With this, you will get to know about the music playing on the video. Clicking on it you will see the name for the track plus the artist info. Alongside this is also a feed to other videos that use the same music for their videos.

After a while you will start to get the hang of the platform and know what works in terms of video engagement and how to tap into this knowledge. You will need a bit of imagination.

When you come across a video that you like very much, you like it by tapping on the love icon to like it just like Instagram and Facebook. And just like Instagram and Facebook, you can engage by leaving comment. The author will pick up on this and you or your brand will be on their rather.

For users to start engaging with your brand, you need consistency and patience.

Following other TikTok Users
If you want to keep up with a great video creator, you can follow them by pressing the icon that includes their profile picture and a plus sign above the heart button on their video.

If you already know of a TikTok account or person that you

want to follow, you can search for them in the search bar and then press the "Users" filter. You can also find them by scanning their TikCode.

This can be helpful for brands or people that want to promote their TikTok channel on other websites or in the physical world. It can also be great if you run into a friend in-person who wants to add you.

To find your own TikCode, go to your profile and tap the icon with four squares in the top right.

To scan another TikCode, go to the search tab and tap the square scan button next to the search bar.

When the scan screen opens, hold it up to the TikCode you want to scan. The scanning process will begin instantly so you don't have to press any other buttons.

Within seconds of a successful scan, you'll be sent to that person's profile. If you have a screenshot of a code, you can also press "Photos" in the top corner of the scan page to upload and scan the code.

It will be wise to following other uses on the platform that has bigger following than you and then engage with the content they are pushing out. Some of those fans will get to see your contribution and some percentage will click over to your profile.

And if they are in the same niche that you want to reach out the better for your brand. That means increased conversion and profits for your brand.

There are actually four ways that you can follow another user on TikTok and the methods vary slightly if you are using an iOS or Android device:

Following TikTok Users on an iOS Device

1. Browse Videos or Categories – When you tap the magnifying class at the bottom of the screen, you will be taken to the page where you can search by category. While on this page, you click on the hashtag or a category that would like to visit. Included at the top of the page also is a search bar. So, when you tap on a video, you can find the profile image in the bottom right conner. Tapping the plus sign will transform it into a check mark.

2. Search for a Username – Again, you can use the magnifying glass to enter the username into the search bar. The user will appear with a "red follow" button at the bottom on the right-hand side. When you tap on it, it will transform into a "white follow" button.

3. Follow contacts on your device – On the screen, you will see a person icon in the far bottom right hand side, tap on the "+" to open it up to the "friends" screen. Now when you tap on the "find contacts friends" you can then follow a contact with the "follow" red button as shown above.

4. Follow Facebook Friends – For this one, you can use the method as described above to get to the friends' screen. When you are there, tap on the "find Facebook friends". You will get a message about signing up to Facebook. So, just tap "continue" You will need to confirm you Facebook login then you are free to invite your friends to Tiktok by using the "red follow" button

Following TikTok Users on an Android Device

1. Follow from Browse – To use your browser to follow someone, you need to open the tiktok and then swipe up the main screen to find an account that you want to follow. Another thing you can do is to look up recent videos by swiping up and down on your home feed. As you swipe, you find the profile pics of user with a red plus sign. Then tapping on this will add you to their followers.

2. Follow from Search – You can tap the magnifying glass icon again. As mentioned above, you can find it at the bottom side of your screen. This will open the search page for you so you can use the search bar at the top to search for other users you can follow. You can also search for sounds and hashtags. So, when the user you want to follow pops up then you just need to tap on the red "follow" button.

3. Follow contacts on your device – On you profile, you just tap on your profile icon at the bottom right screen. This opens the page. Then you need to tap on the person outline with a plus sign in the bottom right hand conner. Next tap on the "Find Contacts Friend". This will scan your phone book. To continue, you need to grant the app access to your phone's contact list so you will tap on the "Allow" prompt. Then you need to tap on the Follow button next to the contact's name you want to follow.

4. Follow Facebook Friends – For Facebook friends, you will need to open your profile page as you did above. Then next, tap on the outline of the person that you wish to follow with the plus sign. This is the same, so you tap on "Find Facebook Friends" Of course you have to sign in to Facebook and grant the app access to your friends. Tiktok scans your friends and pulls up any of your friends that have tiktok accounts. The list will show up and then you can tap on the red "Follow" button.

As a marketer, you have to count on some the people you follow to follow you back and as you get more popular on the bottom others that you are not connected will follow you on their own. This is the reason why you should take great care when crafting your profile bio and the images you use as your profile picture. Also, posting things that will hook people in to follow without following them 1st.

CREATING CONTENT ON TIK-TOK

Types of Posts on TikTok

TikTok is all about video sharing and creating. Besides creating videos of your own, you can do duet on TikTok, create TikTok videos with templates. Explore more fun on TikTok.

Now, let's dive into the kind of videos that you can create on the platform. To do this, we will take a look at the most common types content that are being created on the platform. The key here or should I say the work here is "**entertaining**", so you need to keep that in mind.

Ok, let's go:

Music Videos

It pays to keep in mind that Tiktok is an expansion of the Musical.ly platform. This is crucial because if tiktok is still uses the video format of lip-synch to famous songs. This makes music montages and mini videos to popular on the platform.

There is whole bunch of different lip-synch videos on the platform. TikTok is integrated with video sharing and video creating feature as mentioned above. Creating a TikTok video is extremely easy. So, let's take it step by step-

Step 1- Click on the "+" button. If it is your first time to shoot, you need to allow TikTok to access your camera and recorder.

Step 2- Set up the timer, speed, beauty effects, filters, effects, long press the red button to start shooting.

Step 3- Choose one piece of music to level up your video.

Step 4- Once the film is done, press the red check to go to the editing page.

Step 5- Go to the upper right, you can choose another music, adjust the volume and cut sound.

Step 6- Set one frame of the video as a cover and add other special effects through the two buttons on the down left corner.

Comedy Videos

On the platform, there is bunch that are comedic in nature

and designed to make you laugh. To do this kind videos, you need to put on your creative hat on. There is quite a number of really creative and funny videos on the platform and there is no shortage of talents.

As a marketer marketing for your brand a company, there is no law that say you cannot be funny. In fact, on the contrary, the opposite is the case. It shows the human side of your company and people identify with that.

Most of the videos on the platform are spontaneous and funny. There is no reason why you shouldn't put some thought in creating funny videos of your own. For your brand, you can certainly do spontaneous videos as well. Though this might be a bit tricky to pull off since you are drawing attention to you brand but it's certainly possible.

This not a walk in the park but you should try it, it probably be these kinds of videos that will pull a lot of eyeballs to your page and engage with your brand.

Special Effects Videos

Another kind of videos you can make are videos with special effects. These are the kind of videos that has some filters applied to them. And tiktok has a bunch of these filters on the platform.

As you can imagine, these kinds of videos just as popular as the comedy videos. Once again, your imagination plays an important role here also.

Duet Videos

When it comes to music videos, you can reply to anyone of them by using the "Duet" functionality in TikTok. With this feature you can create your own video right beside the original video using the same music featured on the video. And as you may know, it's pretty cool and it was popular with subscribers in Musical.ly.

You can imagine that some the most popular videos on the

platform are duet videos. So, my theory is that, this feature is the single reason that makes these kinds of videos so popular. And if you make a really cool video on its own and then using the "Duet" feature than your video has the potential to go viral.

There is also the consideration of how other subscribers react to the original video. Of course, some of these reactions might not be what you will expect, that's the nature of social media but this shouldn't stop you.

This is a chance for you to get to know your customers and to produce the kind of videos that they will like and engage with.

Challenge Videos

Another very popular kind of video on Tiktok is a challenge video. And the use of hashtags. This is seen in action when celebrity Jimmy Fallon, the host of tonight show used hashtags to promote his #tumbleweedchallenge.

It was of course with doubt a hit and it went viral. In relatively short time, more than 8000 videos related to this hashtag were posted by people on the platform. The engagement to was off the charts, 10 million!

Challenge videos are not new to social media but everyone can pull them off. If you do manage to pull one off, it's always worth it. These kinds of videos encourages people to participate and to engage in whatever challenge it is.

Another popular challenge is #ChipotleLidFlipChallenge. Here, you are required to flip a Chipotle bowl lid by using the bowl. If you can come up with the right kind challenge then you are sure to have eye balls and engagement on your brand.

Creating a TikTok Video

The key is to put some thought into your videos Don't just jump to making videos without a plan. I recommend making sure that every single piece of video or any content for that matter that you produce have an objective.

That doesn't mean to say that spontaneous videos too don't do well, they do as well, but those are kind of a scatter shot approach. They are unpredictable but when you but some thought into your videos, though this is not a guaranteed, you have a better chance of having a hit in your hands.

Cresting a tiktok video is not really very difficult, it's pretty straight forward. Just like in Instagram and Snapchat, they all have similar features. If you can do that on one platform, then you can do that on the rest. These features are easy to use and very intuitive as well.

So, going into the technical bit, to start with, you have to 1st tap on the plus sign icon located at the bottom of your screen. This opens up your device camera. You will see a large red button for recording your video. Like I stated previously, you make a 15 minute or a 60-minute video.

You can also make a video beforehand and you can use the upload button on the app to upload this video. This way it's easy for you as marketer to plan your video production and beforehand. Though it won't hut to have some couple of off the cuff videos on your page. The finnier the better.

So, whatever way you choose to shoot your video. You can use any of the special effect features to add special effects on the video before publishing it.

Some of these special features are:

- **Speed up your video**
- **Slow down your video**
- **Alternate between your front and back smartphone camera**
- **Add a timer**

To apply any of the several effects on the app, all you need to do is to tap on the "Effect" icon that is located on the left side of your screen. There are several by the way, just browse through them to find any that suits you taste.

As a business, you have made the determination if you will need to feature animals in your videos. Keep in mind though that people will pay attention to how you treat the animals. But there is no doubt that animals have always been and always will be a hit anytime anima pics especially dogs and cats are posted on social media.

For animal videos, there are some special effect you can use to enhance your video. For example, the "beauty" button is especially good to use. You can use this to erase any dark shadows you may have under your eye.

One thing I like tiktok is the way they app is arranged. They had most of the filters numbered and are easy to find unlike Instagram. But the similarity is that both do have these filters to allow you to change the color filter of your camera.

If you the type that likes handsfree recording as much as I do then you will like the timer feature. With this, just as the name suggests, you can record a video hands free.

This helps to give your thumbs a break otherwise you would be holding down the record button for the entire length of the video if you are shooting from within the app itself.

So, I recommend that you spend some time familiarising yourself with the various buttons on the app. Also, try to master the special effects buttons also. This shouldn't take very long for you to master them. Relatively easy to use the app.

Later, you can go into using the duet features and how to apply special effects on them.

Now, when it comes creating a duet video, just tap the share button with the original and then choose duet. As a finishing touch, there is nothing wrong in adding a little bit of music.

This is nothing new by itself. But it's a really neat touch to add your music even after you have uploaded it to recording screen.

To do this, just tap on the "Add a Sound" icon. This located on the right side of your recording screen. A streaming menu of songs and artists will appear similar to Spotify.

Here you can simply brows the most popular tracks on Tiktok that best suits the theme of your message and the ones being used the most on tik-tok by other users. You also will find songs on Apple Music as well.

Just so you know, songs on tiktok are not complete songs but short clips of songs to use in your short videos. And of course, you cannot edit these short clips. They only way to get around this is to play the music on another device while shooting the video on tiktok.

This will register as an original sound. You need to be careful though and pay attention to copyrights of songs if you don't want to be sued. Within the sound's menu, there are tracks associated with Tiktok challenges that you can use.

Once you are done recording this video, tap on the "Next" icon and a page that looks almost like the post page of Instagram will appear. Right on this page, you are allowed to create a caption for your video and as well as add relevant meta data and hashtags.

When done, you can actually add the account handles of other users on Tiktok. And you can also make changes to the privacy settings and enable or disable Duets as you deem fit, turn the comments on or off.

You can also download this video to your smart phone's photo gallery by simply tapping on the "Save to Album" icon. If you don't feel like posting right away, you simply tap on "Draft" this way you can return to it later.

Content Marketing on TikTok

So, just like anything online or social media for that matter, you need to do some marketing as well. This is where you get eye balls to your page.

Once you start creating the kind of content that drive engagement, more people will start to follow you and they will be looking out for more content from you. So, you better have a plan for ramping up your content production to keep them entertained on a regular basis.

On tiktok, there are will be quite a couple of users upload a lot of content constantly onto the platform when they get started and later stop posting regularly after a while. This is not the best way to drive engagement.

This signals to them that you have nothing new to add to offer and they will feel like you don't want to engage with them anymore and they will stop engaging with you as well. This you must avoid at all costs.

Part of your plan is to create a very robust content marketing plan. Aplan for regular posting creation and posting of content. This si something that you need to commit to if you want to successful on tiktok and on social media platforms in general.

New content posted regularly is the only sure way to stay relevant on social media and give your brand the chance at success as you drive up engagement.

TIKTOK HASHTAGS

One thing to note though is that, you need to use relevant hashtags with your tiktok posts. These you can add to your video posts, or any independent posts or on sections for comments. Also, some of the content that post on tiktok can be categorised and this you can do with hashtags.

To use hashtags properly and effectively, this requires that you do a bit of research beforehand. Look at what hangtags has been used in the past that are very popular and trending and just use those. There is no need to try and reinvent the wheel here.

Though that is not to say you cannot create your own hashtags, this is certainly the case when you post goes viral then you just have created a new hangtag associated with your post.

Hashtags also serve a useful purpose also. They let your audience know that the video you uploaded is related to some of your previous posts. This creates a link to those posts. And also, when someone searches using those hashtags, they will all the related posts.

And also, if you want to drive engagement to anything trending you can also use hashtags while posting then on the platform.

Reasons to use TikTok Hashtags

There are quite a number of important reasons for you to use TikTok hashtags especially if you promoting your brand. Here are the two most important reasons:

Get more Likes and Exposure

One of these reasons, which I think really is the most important reason is that this allows your followers or anyone at all interested in the topic to understand what your videos are all about. This will give them a reason to watch and engage.

Like I stated above also, another reasons for search purposes too. People can find your videos using the hashtags you applied to your posts and hence your brand and products.

Another good thing about hashtags, is that they help highlight trending topics on tok-tok. This of course drives up the number of likes that you will get and so helps push your content up the search results on tok-tok. This in turn drives up engagement and also sales of your products.

Increase your Following

On tiktok you can bet that most of the users look for specific kind of content. And they use hashtags as the best way to find these kinds of content. The reason for you to use the most relevant hashtags related to these topics and your content is more likely to appear on the search result pages and be found.

These will help them follow you because you produce something they like. Some uses use popular hashtags on videos and products that are not related to the topic. This is short sided and I will not recommend you follow those approach. Just stick to clean brand marketing and will be glad you did down the line.

How can you find the Best Hashtags for TikTok?

How can you find the best hashtags to use in your posts? You need to know the best way to find the best hashtags for your content on TikTok in such a way that you connect it to your brand as well.

Tricky but not entirely impossible. There are some proven methods that you can focus on to find them:

Know your Audience

Like I said in previous chapters, know you audience. If did you will be able to know tiktok users that are more likely to follow you. The reason being that a lot of these people will only follow certain hashtags on tiktok. Heck I do the same on Instagram!

If you just use random hashtags and you do not categorise

your posts, your brand marketing will not appear coherent. Users will probably ignore your hashtags and your posts. This prevents yiu from establishing authority in your field. So, audience research is something you don't want to mess up.

Conducting good audience research gives you insight into what your audience wants and once you know this, it will easier to for you to create the kinds of content that appeals to them.

As you are planning and creating these contents, you are also need to remember to create your own unique hashtags along the way. And this will boost your brand giving you a feedback loop and then rinse and repeat.

Look at what TikTok Influencers are doing
Part of being successful in anything also involves your ability in adopting proven success strategies from other people. This is no different on tiktok. Just find what the top users are doing and replicating those things. Better still, take those things a bit further.

Do them much better than they are doing those things or find better ways to do them or a spin on any old strategy and see what happens. There is no harm in experimenting a little bit. Just don't go crazy with it and distract your audience since you are on a live account

You also need you be able to read the pulse of the platform, pay attention to trends that these influencers are riding on and the hashtags they are using and do the same. Study their posts, see if there is something there you can apply in your own niche and use to advantage.

Note the hangtags that they are used on their most successful posts and adopt them. Also, look their posts that didn't do so well and see what if anything you can do to make them better and then produce similar posts or avoid the mistakes completely.

Check out your Competitors

I have said this before and I will say it again, spend time on your audience research, don't rush this stage. I have made the same mistake myself so don't do the same. This gives you the ability to see the hashtags that the big dogs are using and adapt them to your particular niche.

How important this stage is cannot be over emphasised, so, take you time especially if your brand is new to the platform. By the way, this applies not just tiktok alone but all social media platforms. Take a look at successful pages and simply copy what they do and adapt them to your niche.

Granted some of their strategies or hashtags will not be successful in your niche but that's alright just keeping searching that angle that has the potential to propel your brand. It's out there just have a little patience.

Use Tools to find good TikTok Hashtags

To make your work easy, there are good tools that you can use to find hashtags. Using these tools properly will show you popular hashtags for specific niches. Here are a couple of good tools that your competitors are using and you can use them too:

Seekmetrics

Seekmetrics is a nice little tool that you can use to find really popular hashtags that are trending on tiktok. The tools have the ability for you to measure your performance on the platform giving you ideas for improvement.

Seekmetrics has a search feature that allows you to type in a hashtag keyword and the software will spit out some suggestions for you to analyse. Just copy these suggestions and add them to your posts and videos.

It's quite easy to use and it has a nice interface that is very intuitive and smooth. Try it out and see how that affects your bottom line in weeks.

All Hashtag

What is **AllHashtags**? This another good hashtag finder that you can deploy. Just like Seekmeytrics, it's easy to use. Just type in a hashtag keyword and the software will do the rest for you. It also has the ability to pull up related hangtags. You will them all in the results.

This is cool because you don't have to go research related hashtag keywords separately. The only thing it's a bit hard trying to separate all the keywords. So, like above, just copy these hashtags and apply them to your particular niche.

The Best 100 Hashtags to use for more Likes

Here are some of the best hashtags that we recommend you use to get more likes for your TikTok posts. This is by no means an exhaustive list but it is a good start, And, also you need to apply them according your own niche:

1. #tiktok
2. #funny
3. #love
4. #followme
5. #memes
6. #cute
7. #music
8. #fun
9. #fashion
10. #happy
11. #musically
12. #follow
13. #followforfollowback
14. #comedy
15. #lol
16. #meme
17. #like4like
18. #muser
19. #video
20. #girl

21. #funnyvideos
22. #dankmemes
23. #dance
24. #likeforfollow
25. #tbt
26. #tiktokindo
27. #me
28. #repost4follow
29. #summer
30. #picoftheday
31. #friends
32. #life
33. #beauty
34. #life
35. #selfie
36. #smile
37. #amazing
38. #family
39. #beach
40. #ootd
41. #beautiful
42. #fitness
43. #sky
44. #pretty
45. #foodporn
46. #sunset
47. #dog
48. #hair
49. #swag
50. #vsco
51. #cat
52. #makeup
53. #holiday
54. #inspiration
55. #iphoneonly
56. #sea

57. #fashion
58. #art
59. #tagsforlikes
60. #sun
61. #nofilter
62. #travel
63. #followforfollow
64. #photo
65. #photography
66. #vscocam
67. #model
68. #photography
69. #instalike
70. #nature
71. #nyc
72. #photooftheday
73. #home
74. #drawing
75. #healthy
76. #bestoftheday
77. #gym
78. #baby
79. #design
80. #cool
81. #instapic
82. #motivation
83. #night
84. #party
85. #instacool
86. #christmas
87. #fit
88. #goodmorning
89. #workout
90. #blue
91. #flowers
92. #handmade

93. #blackandwhite
94. #instafood
95. #yummy
96. #pink
97. #hot
98. #lifestyle
99. #work
100. #black

Take a careful look at these hashtag suggestions and sort through them to find those that best suits your niche and your kind of posts. As you can see, some of them are general so you can experiment with these.

Always, remember that you should measure your hashtag performance, this is crucial as it is very important for your success on the TikTok platform.

HOW TO USE HASHTAGS EFFECTIVELY ON TIKTOK

Getting hashtags is one thing but using them properly is entirely a different thing. So, here are some hashtags best practices you can use:

1- Don't stuff your hashtags. Just looking a hashtag and it is long, it will loose its power because it will no longer be interesting. Just like domain names. Long domain names are not memorable so the shorter the better.

2- Don't stuff too many hashtags in your posts. Just like it's not counterproductive to stuff your website content with too many keywords. Anyway, Tiktok has set a limit of 100 characters which includes hashtags and spaces as well.

3- Also, you need to know when is the right time to post your hashtag content to ensure maximum visibility.

Below is a chart from Influencer Marketing Hub on a study they conducted that shows optimal times for posting content on Tiktok-

Global Best Times to Post on TikTok
Eastern Standard Time

Monday	Tuesday	Wednesday	Thursday	Friday	Saturday	Sunday
	2 AM			5 AM		
6 AM	4 AM	7 AM				7 AM
	9 AM	8 AM	9 AM		11 AM	8 AM
10 AM			12 PM			
				1 PM		
			7 PM	3 PM	7 PM	4 PM
10 PM		11 PM			8 PM	

"Best times to post as calculated by Influencer Marketing Hub after analyzing more than 100,000 global TikTok posts and engagement rates."

The study also found that there are certain factors that impact posting times.

1- 1. Audience Location

This makes sense because you want to post content at a time that a particular region is awake and online. The zones are come into play here and you should pay attention to it.

2- Audience Awake Time

Once you know where your audience is located, find out the times when they are up and running. This is a little tricky.

For example, if your audience is split between the UK and Australia, there's a time gap of approximately 9 hours between these two zones. You need to schedule your content in such a way that you can reach audiences in both countries.

Unfortunately, TikTok doesn't have a built-in scheduling feature. However, you can use social media posting and scheduling tools that line up your content in advance and post them automatically at the right time.

MARKETING STRATEGIES FOR TIKTOK

Now we are getting int the meat and potatoes, **Tiktok Brand Marketing Strategies**. I believe that there are three ways that you can effectively market your brand on TikTok:

1. **You create your own branded channel and upload relevant videos for your niche**
2. **You can identify and work with influencers on TikTok to increase your reach on the platform**

3. **You can advertise on TikTok (we will cover this in the next chapter).**

One thing that I want to point out is that most tiktok users use a combination of these hashtags to grow their pages and hence their brands. In the next chapter, I will talk about the most successful marketing strategies that many brands have adopted and are still using right now.

1. Hashtag Challenges

Challenges are very popular on tiktok. And it's not at all difficult to start one. Thing is starting one that a lot of people will identify with. This is the only way to make it go viral and boost your brand.

Because of the funny and interesting nature of challenges, a lot of tiktok users like to accept them. If you are lucky enough to have one that celebrities adopt then you are going make a killing with sales of your products.

So, I recommend that you try all you can to create a challenge on tiktok. To this, you need to start off with finding an exciting hashtag and relevant hashtag. Your hashtag needs to be both of these things if you ever going to stand a chance of having a successful challenge.

As I have already mentioned previously the impact of celebrity power like Jimmy Fallon can be if they adopt your challenge. Yes of course he has the celebrity power and the Tonight Show Platform, this shouldn't stop you because you don't have one.

But assuming we take out the celebrity status, the challenge was still a good run. It generated over 8000 videos created by other users and over 10 million engagements in a short period.

He simply asked the tiktok community to drop to the ground and roll like a tumbleweed when they hear a particular piece of music. It's funny and not many people will be willing to do something relatively daring and that's why it's called a challenge.

Part of the ability to have a challenge that goes viral is your ability to read your audience and gauge what they will love to engage with the most on tiktok.

You can make it so that they are required to hold one of your products and do something funny with it. And also note that the more difficult, daring and funny it is the better chance of t going viral.

So, I suggest that you make it as difficult as humanly possible so that people are driven to give it a go. Whatever you do, think about your audience safety as well. You want to something that they can do that is safe and healthy.

For the example I cited about the Jimmy Fallon challenge, the difficulty there was the rolling like a tumbleweed part because you have to do it in public for everyone to see. Not everyone will be comfortable doing that in the streets.

Those that did were happy that they were able to overcome their shyness of doing something seemingly silly in public.

One thing though I would like to point out is that it's always a good idea to make it a bit flexible and allow tiktok users and anyone who wants to take up the challenge a bit more interesting and those who ordinarily won't have the stomach for it to participate.

Or the ability for participants to put there one spin on it. They can make it as difficult as they want or as easy as its comfortable for them

One notable example is the jeans company GUESS. They really hit a homerun with this in one of the promotions. As you know a lot more people ware the jeans more than they wear any other outer garment.

So, in their challenge, they encouraged tiktok users and anyone willing to participate to show off how they like to wear their favourite jeans. This gave people the freedom to adopt and experiment and as well as use filters and other special effects within tiktok in their videos.

One other powerful brand that used a challenge effectively is Google. Their challenge is focused on Google Assistant. Just think about it, there is absolutely nothing that you cannot ask Google Assistant.

So, what did they do? They invited folks to ask any question that they wanted of the device. This as you must have imagined made the whole challenge very creative and popular. Needless to say, it went viral. Of course, part of it was the brand power of Google but you get the point.

2. Use Duets

Duets are another popular thing on tiktok as mentioned in previous chapters. You have to use this as much as possible with your brand. You have to find good and relevant hashtags to create your campaign.

Part of the challenge of creating a challenge (no pun intended) is that you need to make it unique as much as you can and creative to attract a great deal of engagement form tiktok users.

The well-known DJ Khaled, if you don't know is now an official Tiktok partner. His twist on duets is that he created the hashtag #Catchtheseblessings. He just simply created duets where he is looking at himself and praising other people.

So, if you want to join in on the fun, all you need to do is to use the Duet function on tiktok to record yourself beside DJ Khaled and react to what he is saying in his video.

So, I encourage you to think about other ways in which you can engage with your audience and followers using the Duet feature in TikTok. Remember, make it fun, and interesting.

Here are some ideas:

- **Sing to one another**
- **Hold a conversation**
- **High five each other**
- **Finish each other's sentences**

These are not the only ways you can use Duets, so use your imagination, be creative and ask people around you or your staff for ideas. Get them involved in the process. Believe me this works all the time. Tiktok users like the duet feature so capitalise on this and run with it.

If you get this right, you can bet that you will see sales rolling in like you never imagined before because you are driving a ton of engagement to your brand and products,

3. Use Influencers

Influencers usually pop up on any social media. If they are not there yet, just give it time. These are power users, people that adopted the platform early on and latched on to it. In time they created this following so huge that you cannot simply ignore them.

Tiktok is no exception when it comes to having a top influencer. But the difference here is that the Tiktok platform don't have a lot of influencers at the moment compared to say for example Instagram. In China maybe a bit more but in the Sates not so much.

As stated in the section on Tiktok stats, the platform is relatively new especially in the US. And you know, the US market is just as big as the Chinese market. So, finding them should be easy.

And if you work really hard. Your brand can become one too. And you can smile all the way to the bank.

You better believe it when I say that even though the platform is new, there are influencers there that have millions of followers already. That shows you just how popular the platform is and the rate of adoption of the app.

These influencers can also help with your marketing. Get them to promote your product and your brand. This of course will cost you. It's all a part of your marketing budget.

If you decide to go this route, make sure that the influencer you pick has the authenticity to their page. And that the content they post is in line with your brand and product.

You don't want to be promoting a harvesting tractor on a page that only talks about nursing mothers and new born babies. This example is a bit out there but you get the point.

Other big brands like Google have used influencers in the past to spread the word about their campaigns and boos their brand effectively. And they will continue to do so. And you should do the same as well. Only you need to play the game with the level that your marketing budget permits.

There are quite a couple of successful influencers marketing other brands very well using hashtags and challenges that we talked about earlier on. Also have to be flexible enough to give them a bit of room.

They know their audience and they what gets them excited so giving them a chance to have impute in how the challenge and any content you might want to sue in your campaign is created is probably a good idea.

Don't impose everything on them give them room to make adjustments where necessary while maintaining your brands core values.

Whatever you do, make site that the influencer is comfortable with your brand 1st and that they are just put for the money they will get. This way they are invested in your brand and contributing positively. This is a win-win for everyone, for your brand and as well as their own brand.

Always keep in mind that there a lot younger people on the Tiktok platform and plan and design your campaigns accordingly.

4. Use Scarcity

Another strategy you can adopt is scarcity. Yes, it works very well. This has been used since the internet became a thing and will continue to be effective.

Just like any platform, scarcity also works on Tiktok. So, since you are all about encouraging engagement and participation from your users, having a bit of time constraints never huts. It helps to push Tiktok users to take action on your products quickly.

The reason being that someone who might be sitting on the fence will be pushed to take action quicker so they don't miss the offer.

So, creating a challenge with some form of time limit to it is very effective. When uses know this, they are forced to take action and join in on the challenge quickly.

For example, the earlier example I talked about, GUESS. The company gave users of the platform 7 days to participate and complete the challenge. This moved a lot of people to participate and not put it off. This as you can imagine drove engagement through the roof for the brand.

5. Be Authentic

Authenticity is something that is vital to any branding no matter the social media platform that you choose. But with tiktok, it is particularly important because it's a new platform and not saturated at the moment with big brands like it it with Instagram or Facebook and other.

So quicker you get onboard the better for your company and brand because it will eventually be dominated by big brands.

When you are on any social media platform, whether it's Facebook, Pinterest or Instagram, you need to be yourself, be authentic, that way people will connect to easily. The same goes for Tiktok even more so than another platform.

People can smell a phony mile away and you will have no engagement if you are not yourself and authentic. And again, don't be sales oriented all the time. Try being nice and friendly with nothing attached once in a while.

Try to encourage a sense of community and creativity, that way when you are ready to sell, your followers can buy easily from you.

Engagement with your brand should such that it can be away that your followers can use to get likes and shares the rest of the community. Encourage engagement on their peoples pages as well. Don't horde your followers, encourage them to visit other people's pages as well.

This will encourage others to ask their followers to visit your page as well.

6. Build a Community

Going on Tiktok as a way to promote your brand should be an all-in affair. I see it as all or nothing kind of mind set. You should be prepared to build a long-lasting community.

So, when you are working on creating a challenge, don't see it as one-off campaign, take at as something that you will need to be doing often. Like I said, like it or not you need a budget of marketing and I encourage you to add Tiktok marketing in your marketing budget.

Just for s start, unless you have a seasoned marketer, I suggest you start with making simple short videos. Don't go something fancy. Jut simple and punchy will do just fine. Maybe use some of those filters I talked about a little. And as you get familiar with the platform and they things work; you can start to dive a little deeper.

Another thing is the tone of your whole presentation. You should endeavour to establish this from the start. And once you have established this, never change it for any reason, no matter what. Your videos should also reflect this tone.

For example, is your tone going to be funny, controversial, or positive?

7. Encourage User Generated Content

When it comes to other new generations, they engage differently on social media. Take for instance the generation Z crowd, they would like to be completely emersed in their social network of choice.

These are people that you would see more on their phone even when they are sitting in a café with friends. They would prefer to playing video games rather than watching TV. This is of course passive for it to be entertaining.

When you present this opportunity for them to engage without limits and without restrictions you will have won them over. More eye balls on your brand and more sales of course down the line.

The point here is that, all you do is to encourage Titok users to like, comment and share your videos. There must be a reason for them to any one of these things. Give it to them and stand back, they would do the rest.

The same goes with your products, because you set the tone

and the kind engagement you want from them. So, when you post a video for a challenge or duet, they would do the same.

Look, creating an engaging community on Tiktok is no walk in the park. It needs continuous commitment for a period of time. Stick with it and you would be rewarded.

Let me tell you about a little-known restaurant in China. This restaurant, decided to add a DIY option on their menu. Imagine giving people the option to come to your kitchen and allow them to cook whatever they want to eat. Pretty awesome right?

Of course, it is! These guys that decided to take the restaurant up on its offer turned this to something really spectacular, they made videos of themselves cooking unique dishes. These videos where uploaded to the Chinese version of Titok, Douyin.

What do you think happed to some these videos? They went viral of course and they got publicity like no other. The restaurant experienced one of its strongest growth periods since they opened.

In-fact, people started asking the restaurant to allow them to create their on-DIY options. A further 15,000 plus customers were involved. And even less than half those made videos and shared them, that's massive publicity right there.

Records show that over 50 million users viewed these videos. And that, my friend is marketing at its best.

8. Promote your Videos on other Social Channels

One good thing about creating videos for Tiktok is that, that same video can be used on other platforms. There is no rule that say you cannot do this. Post them on your website as well and cross promote everything.

This way, you pull traffic from Tiktok to website or blog. Either way you make your business more popular with each video or duet that post.

TIK-TOK ADS

When it comes to ads, Tiktok hasn't pushed ads to all countries. So, do your own research. But one country to have started this early on was the US. To know if ads placement is available where you live, please go to https://ads.tiktok.com.

The platforms ads started to show up in January 2019. But a little later in April 2019, Tiktok launched a version where you are allowed to manage your ads by yourself in beta. In this version, you can bead on it just as other marketers can.

I don't know long the reps who run these ads for will continue to do so. It probably will change in the future. So, let's talk a little bit about Tiktok ads and the types of ads that are available on Tiktok platform.

The designers of the ads section of the app made it in such a way that you can only use an in-feed video ad. This makes a whole lot of sense because videos on the platform are only short videos clips.

But you also have 3 different models to choose from:

1. Cost Per Click (CPC)
2. Cost Per Thousand Impressions (CPM)
3. Cost Per View (CPV) – this is a 6 second view

Audience targeting is simple enough to understand. You can decide to go for male or female gender targeting or age or even geo targeting at state levels. That's talking about the US market now.

The platform, has plans to introduce other targeting options like behaviour, interests and even go deeper to the granular levels.

Not sure what if any experience you have with ads on any social media platform. But you will do better when you make ad budget big enough that it allows you to turn a profit. This is the same advice that Tiktok gives to advertisers on the platform.

There are a couple of integrations that the platform is working in terms of placing ads. For example, integration with CRM isn't available yet. Hence you need to use a physical list. Of course, as the platform develops, you are sure to see self-ad service option and a range of other useful integrations.

Brand Takeover Ads

There are a couple of things you can do when setting up ads. One of them is the brand takeover option. This is a way for you to make your ad appear as soon as someone opens tok-tok. This is very good since it allows you to drive traffic to an external page which could be anything you like.

On the ad platform, just one adviser is allowed to use a brand takeover per ad per category in a single day. This am sure will change with time in the as the platform evolves. What this does is that it probably will make the ads expensive.

For users, you can decide to skip the ad and you can do that using the button at the top of the screen.

As brand take over ads go, you are able to measure the reach of your ads by looking at the click through rates, unique clicks and impressions.

Of course, you are placing effective that are designed to be user friendly and to have an impact on your audience. So, I hope you put some thoughts into it.

The Hashtag Challenge Ad

With hashtag challenges, you aim is to drive engagement. To encourage users to generate content with your request from them to participate in the challenge. Of course, as they do this, it puts your brand front and centre on Tiktok.

As mentioned previously, challenges are very popular on Tiktok and will remain so for the next foreseeable future so why not cash in in while the wave lasts. If you are able to get just right then you can expect some really nice results.

The reasons that these kinds of challenges are successful is because they capitalize of an average Tiktok use to want to create their own content or make things interesting for themselves and the people around them.

If you decide to create a hashtag challenge ad, a representative from Tiktok will be there to help you and guide through it all. Up to about 6 days since that's the length of a typical ad on the platform.

When you are promoting your challenge, if you reach out to a good influencer who is well known then, you challenge will be really popular. This will help you reach more people because people always want to identify with people they admire and influencers have that kind power.

If you hit on the right kind challenge, this result in a huge increase in engagement organically and drive some sales for your product or service.

Branded Lens Ads

These are similar to the AR Lenses offered by Instagram and Snapchat. The concepts are not so different when you analyse them. Some these branded lens apps helps you to see 3D objects, face filters and much more.

When you adopt this, a branded lens provides a higher level of engagement on TikTok which in turn drives sales. And with a good user base support, the better your outcomes will be in your sales numbers.

In Feed Native Ads

On Instagram, their story ads are full screen and if this appeals to your audience on that that platform then the Tiktok feed native ads will play well with them on Tiktok as well. On Tiktok, you are allowed to add a link to your products and services on your website.

And just like other on other platforms, the feed native also comes with the ability for users to skip the ad if they want.

These types of ads are designed with a number of design options that you can choose from. Any design you decide to go with, you have the ability to measure the level of engagements you get with this ad type. These includes, viewing times, click through rates and impressions.

With in-feed native ads, your ads can be between 5 to 15 seconds in length. You are required to make the video in a vertical format and it displays on the "For Your" page of your users tiktok page.

The platform allows you to place some calls to action on the page too, allowing users to visit your website and take action on your products and services.

The ads on the platform is the best in terms of usability but there is hope and room for improvement. I have confidence that things will improve for sure because that's how the platform makes its money and they need to make it as easy as possible for business.

Of course, at this point you can't expect the level of sophistication you see Facebook ads platform or Instagram for that matter, but it will get better with time. They have no choice but to make it so.

Due to this reason, ads on the platform will remain as cheap as they can allow it for now and for good reason too.

They want as many businesses as possible to get on the [platform and start using the app. The more business they get on it the better they can monetize the app and the better their bottom line.

And the sooner you get onboard the better for your brand. The platform already has enough user base to make your ad investments worth your while.

If you are familiar with other ad platforms on other social media companies, you will know that it's a good idea to change things up, mix and match things up when you designing your ads.

And make room for testing ads against other ads of your own and those of other marketers as well. You need to be able to figure out why a particular is performing or under performing and tweak and improve until you get an optimal result.

Of course, part of ad design is that you need to make sure that they stand out just enough to be noticed and not as sore thumb. Nobody likes sore thumbs so make sure that your ads blend in nicely with Tiktok platform as much as you can.

Usually the reps make suggestion to things like color and typography to help you get up and running quickly as possible. Even when they ads platform goes self-serving, any ads you put up will still require approval before its allowed to go live.

Yes, it might seem like a lot to learn and do with Tiktok and ads but I promise you that if you stick with it, you will glad you did down the road. Most of the best performing ads are usually entertaining and consistent with your message.

So, pay attention to planning before you deploy ads. Better well planned and executed few than lots of ads that are so generic that they are lost in the me-too category.

TIKTOK USE CASES TO INSPIRE YOU

On this section, I want to talk about business that have seen some success on Tiktok even though the platform is relatively new on the scene. As you already, when platforms like this comes along, the early adopters stand to benefit the most.

Usually new platforms see really faster growth then the older platforms. On Tiktok, some of the early users includes; sports teams. Some celebrities in the film industry, musicians, collage athletes and as well some business.

And of course, not forgetting that some late show hosts like Jimmy Fallon also where one of the people to get in on the platform early on.

The Bailey Bakery
One of the things that make Tiktok so good is that its highly demonstrative and showy in a nice way. So, any business has its nature is demonstrative will do very well. Say for example, bakeries, and Pastry makers and as well cake decorators.

As you know it's hard to talk about cooking any exotic dish without a video. So comes Baily Bakery. It's a real joy with high quality video to see them do thing and of course, Tiktok users eat it all up every time.

If you go in the platform and search for these types business and as individual chefs, lots of them have amassed followers of up to 100,000 plus on Tiktok and counting. On this count, the Baily Bakery really stands out.

There followers are over 4 million and counting at the time of this writing. Their video engagement is through the roof, receiving over 90 million likes across all of their videos.

Their videos of course are professionally shot and they showcase bakers decorating cookies and other stuff while the music plays in the background. Talk about marketing per excellence. And they sometimes employ the speed effect when appropriate.

Anthony Barbuto Lawyer
One other example that still surprises everyone including me is that of a lawyer. You remember that the platform is suited more to business that are showy in a way and that's far from law.

But Anthony Barbuto managed to find a way to make it for his law practice. And it turns out its just him alone. There are quite a few others getting good results on the platform. So, you have no excuses whatsoever.

With Anthony, has got over 1.8 million followers and most of his videos has got over 26 million likes across the board. And he is not the only lawyer on Tiktok. There is quite a handful of them.

They simple share their thoughts and ideas on the platform and these resonate with people quite a bit hence the level of engagement.

University of Florida
And of course, when you talk about universities and colleges, you think of the younger generation, a generation that almost live their entire on their mobile. No wonder some universities and colleges are doing well on the platform.

The university of Florida is one that stands out to me. The school has got more than 83,000 followers and almost a million likes for all the videos they have posted so far. And of course, this will only keep growing if they maintain what they are doing.

They are able to achieve this impressive result because they leveraged what they already have to build a following on the platform. And that is students and a really nice setting for videos and images. So, they give you people the chance to see behind the scenes of the campus and everything.

Everything from the look of the campus grounds, videos of their football and other sports teams and as well as dance challenges. It's not difficult for these students to shoot and the school can really take the best and publish on the university website.

Lis Nas X

For musicians, it's easy for them because their business model is all about show. This is perfect for a Tiktok platform. One notable Tiktok user is Lil Nas X, a rapper that really shot up Tiktok search pages like crazy.

His Old Town Road song as heavily promoted using Tiktok and it was massive success. You see, he was relatively an unknown singer but when you dived into Tiktok he exploded into people's rather.

His song went viral on the platform and has become one the go to reference as what you can do with the Tiktok platform by targeting the cool kids on there. The song also became an all-time number 1 hit song and longest running hit song on Billboard 100 and as well as Spotify.

He was able to achieve this by simply posting a video him performing the song on Tiktok. The song was quickly turned into a meme and the rest as you must have guessed was history.

The song got picked up by so many Tiktok users that it produces over 500 million views shattering long held records and it also resulted in over 5 million users making videos around his hashtag #oldtownroad.

The Lomile Shop

Even folks with ecommerce stores are no exception. If you do have one, you can be doing well if you applied yourself to Tiktok. The small ecommerce players are seeing success on the platform promoting their products on there.

So, the way they do this is by creating and uploading videos that show how the products work while playing a music at the background. This is relatively easy to do and if you are just starting out with Tiktok, you don't need to make it so professional.

For the brand Lomile, they didn't do anything spectacularly different. They just created a video that walks you through one of their products that you can use to organise your closet. That's it simple product review and it received nearly 2 million likes and about 7000 comments.

Think about, imagine if you tried making your video a bit more exciting, what that can mean to your company and to your bottom line.

The Washington Post
The Washington Post, yes even them too are on Tiktok. When I 1st read about this, I didn't think that they will be on Tiktok too. They have if am not mistaken a different kind of audience. This goes to show that the demographic is changing on the platform or better still expanding.

The Washington Post has close to around 160,000 followers on the platform. They have contents on their page that has generated 4 million hearts or likes if you will. The company employ the features that are freely available to every Tiktok user very well.

Talk about knowing all you can about the platform that you on. There will be tricks that you might not be aware of. They use these features very well when they create their content. They have decided to embrace the fun and the meme nature of the platform to fullest.

What they have done is to provide some videos with the behind the scenes of their news room and some their cast members.

For example, they posted a video with a fun exchange between one of their reporters and the editor that has become one the most viewed videos. It generated over 100,000 hearts and incredible 160 comments.

The Pasco County Sheriff's Office

How about law enforcement? You bet, them too are all in on the fun. They don't want to leave all the fun to the kids. Lots of individual cops have started their accounts including an entire sheriff's offices.

Like it or hate it, they have drawn some really nice comments with their posts. One of such law enforcement offices to latch on to the trend of Tiktok is The Pasco County Sheriff's Office.

Their posts have attracted about 300,000 followers with of 3 million hearts and counting daily. Why not, it's fun to be in the action with these officers as they create ride along videos and post them on the platform.

Behind the scenes clips of especially with a Sheriff's office and deputies will always attract a lot views and likes. They too know how to do funny to say the least. Who wouldn't like to see a deputy in uniform taking up dance challenges eh?

Other Success Stories

If you go on to the platform, am sure you can find a thousand other successful stories like these. And there will be many more to come as the platform matures and becomes more popular.

Take for example, the MBA. They have a presence on the platform with over 5.5 million followers, 79 million likes on their posts. Their strategy is to post different kinds of content on the platform from highlights of basketball matches to fans dancing.

Most of the teams on NBA also have their Tiktok accounts and they simply post as they wish. A notable one is the Chicago Bulls. They also have an account just for their mascot with the name "Benny the Bull" can you imagine. The mascot Benny also has an Instagram account as well.

The mascot Benny makes collaboration videos with other mascots. You can imagine just funny these videos will be. One of their most popular videos was with the mascot form Philadelphia Flyers with the name Gritty.

This also tells me that the platform offers many opportunities for co*marketing with other brands no matter how small. All you need is the courage to get out there and do you thing.

These are stories that you should use as motivation to get on the platform. If they can do it, why not you? You can learn and adapt. It shouldn't be that heard. You have seen companies big and small so you too can do well on there.

TIKTOK ANALYTICS

There is now you can talk about marketing your brand without talking about Analytics and measurable results. That's what we are going to be talking about here on this section. Tracking analysing, and measuring can be the difference between your success and failure.

You need to know when something is working well for your campaigns and to double down on it or stop when something is not working. That's where Analytics, tracking and measurement come in.

You will need a Pro Account

Just as you have on Instagram, what they call Instagram Creator account, Tiktok has recently unveiled their Native Analytics Program. This is only available to pro users only.

On this feature, you can use the analytics (I discussed earlier) dashboard on Tiktok to discover insights about your audience, the behavioural patterns and how you're the contents that you publish is doing.

On Tiktok, you will find that it's easy to switch from basic to pro account. To do this, just go to your profile settings then you need to tap the "Manage My Account" icon. Then when the next screen opens up, tap on "Switch to Pro Account".

The next step is to choose the category you want your account to be. Then the finale step you need to enter your mobile phone number from which you can receive your verification code via SMS. Once you get that, then you need to enter the code and then that's it.

So, to see your page analytics, you will need to go back to the settings menu and you will find Analytics. When you tap on this, you will be taken to your dashboard. You can now select the pro account.

Your activities and records will be displayed on the dashboard but you need to switch to the pro account for those records to be displayed.

It usually takes about a week for data to show up on the dashboard and that will be in line to the amount of activities you have engaged in on the platform. So, to start analysing your results you need to post as much as possible within this one week.

There are three categories on your TikTok analytics dashboard which are:

1. **Profile overview**
2. **Content insights**
3. **Follower insights**

To take a closer, all you need do it tap on the tabs at the top of the screen and select the categories you want to take a look at.

The Profile Overview

On the profile, you are able to see just how well your account is performing since you started using the platform. This page shows the total profile views for all time. You will also see your total view on all your video broken for you plus your total followers.

On the page, you will notice that your video views are displayed 1st showing you the total number of times users have viewed your videos with the last 7 days or 28 days.

Not only that, there is break down of the daily views too. This will help you to know the peak days and time, giving you ideas on the best time to post on the platform.

Another thing you will see also is that your profile views are broken down much the same way as your video views. The same 7 day and 28-day option and also broken down into individual days for deeper analyses.

These data and metrics are so very important. For you to grow you audience, know them better and be in a better position to offer them the best service. That means you have all you need to design a better marketing campaign and content strategy for your brand.

As data on your usage and audience activities keeps growing, you will start to see a pattern emerge on your audience activities and Tiktok usage. It helps you make better and informed decisions on your marketing.

Content Insights

In your account, you can also get a really good insight on your content from the content tab within the Tiktok analytics page. They are broken down from the newest to the oldest within the last week giving you a bird's eye view of your performance on the platform.

On this page, you can see a couple of other things-
- You will get to see which of all the videos you posted so far has trended on the "For You" page for the same period.
- You will also see the total views for all these videos for all the process.

The great thing about this how they are all broken down into individual video performance is that you get to see how each particular video or post performed. You can duplicate that to get more of the same results.

When you study your analytic, you will get the following metrics for each post:

- **Total hearts (likes) for the post**
- **Total comments for the post**
- **Total shares for the post**
- **Total video play time**
- **Total video views**
- **The Average watch time**
- **Sources of traffic**

- **Audience territories**

Under the audience metrics, you will be able to see which of your post resonated the best with which segment of your audience and like I said before you can replicate that kind content and rinse and repeat.

This data is presented neatly by country and region. This gives you a chance to compare regions and the kind of content that does well with each of the regions.

Follower Insights

To see the insight about demographics you go into the Follow Insights section. The page is divided into male and female sections and also broken down into percentages per section. The regions are broken down to country levels as well.

Pentos TikTok Analytics Tool

All I have talked about so far is looking at analytics of your account to see how you are performing at any given time. But you know you also need info on how your competitors are doing so you can better manage your expectations.

Unfortunately, as of now, there is no way of peeking into your competitor's performance with Tiktok platform. So, how do you do this? You will need a 3rd party analytic tool.

There is an external analytics tool provided by **Pentos** for Tiktok users. There probably other out there but for now this is a good start. This will help you gather publicly available Tiktok profile data and analyse them in real time.

It's important that you know just before you sign up for free that the data is not directly from the Tiktok app itself. They website makes it clear that the data they gather is only from the Tiktok website only. So, bear that in mind as you use the tool.

The website has a free version and as you might have guessed, it's limited on the amount of data you can pull up. So, for a more in-depth analysis you might want to upgrade to a premium account level.

There are 2 levels here. The $19 a month level and the $99 a month level.

Looking in the Pentos dashboard you can see the following for each account you are tracking:

- **The average engagement rates**
- **Total number of hearts**
- **Total number of video posts**
- **The average number of hearts (likes)**
- **The average number of comments**
- **The number of other TikTok accounts that the profile follows**

Pentos can be used for a variety of research targets. For example, if you wanted to find the right influencer covering a particular segment of your audience, you can Pentos to find them.

With Pentos also, you can see what the influencer's average engagement rate is and how effective the influencer can be for your campaign.

With the premium version you can do a much more. For example, you can find hashtags to use in your posts and just how good or popular the hashtag is. This is displayed on the hashtag challenge dashboard and within it you can find the following:

- **The average hashtag engagement rate**
- **The average number of comments**
- **The total views to the hashtag content**
- **Total number of posts using the hashtag**
- **The average likes for the hashtag**

When it comes to Tiktok marketing, Pentos can come in handy and help you run business with ease. Of course, there are other marketing tools that you can deploy for your business. It's a good idea to just start with the free version of Pentos then upgrade as your need for more insight grows.

This is good if you are short on cash. Whether free or not you have a bit of an edge over other marketers that don't know this exist.

TIKTOK BEST PRACTICES

Even though the Tiktok platform is relatively new on the scene, and it doesn't have a lot of things figured out yet doesn't mean you should ignore it. On the contrary, this the very reason that you should be get on there as quickly as possible.

This way you will be better positioned to capitalize on the growth and adoption of the platform as the years pass by.

When it comes to marketing, a lot of marketers have already had success on the platform and many have figured out a couple of things through their experimenting on the platform. Here are a couple of the best Tiktok practices that you can adopt for your campaigns:

1. TikTok has a young User Base

When you look at the generation Z folks on Tiktok, what do you see? They want to entertain and or be entertained as well as participate in that entertainment. So, 1st rule of marketing and sales, give people what they want.

You can't go wrong if you applied this rule. As I stated previously, the demographics on Tiktok will continue to grow and change but for the moment, the generation Z folks dominate the platform so always keep this in mind as you plan out you content strategy.

2. Always use Music

Still in the spirit of giving consumers what they want; on Tiktok, users have grown accustomed to having music with the videos they view so give it to them.

Just for reminders, its important to remember that most of those users came over form Musical.ly where they are used to seeing videos with background music and is dominant on the platform. So, they will be looking out for such content on Tiktok platform.

3. Use the Special Effects

Like I started, producing your videos can be daunting sometimes but you shouldn't let that stop you. You can make your videos exciting in various ways and the special effects features that I talked about in previous chapters.

The keyword here is knowing all you can about these features and how best to apply them on your contents. Obviously experiment until you find the optimal blend of features on your videos. And do keep an eye out for how other brands are applying these features.

4. Use Multiple Shots in your Videos

If I may suggest, you might try making videos with multiple shots stitched together. It could be quite nice and interesting if done properly. Of course, all your videos should be like these. Just keep experimenting and find how your followers react to them.

5. Challenge your Audience

For users on the platform, they enjoy challenges and that's why you see that hashtag challenges on the platform are very popular. With this in mind, if you created a challenge to promote your brand then you should come up with a really nice hashtag to go with the challenge.

Most people simply use the name or the title of their challenge as the hashtag it makes it easier. Just think of ways to make it interesting and fun. And also make sure you set a deadline for your challenge especially if the goal is to market a certain product or services.

6. Take a look at your Competitors

Like always, to be competitive, you need info on your competitors. So, go get them. Analyse their strategy, the content format and generally all you can about them.

This is so you do better things they are doing poorly or do thing they are not doing at all. This info can also give you ideas of your own that you apply in your campaigns. It's not good nor is it ethical to copy what they are doing outright.

Simply take their methods and strategies and apply your own spin on them.

7. Use Analytics

Always use analytics, you cannot make decisions at least to for very long and not effectively just by eyeballing your user engagement. You need to use good tools that can help you and save you time also.

All content you post will not go viral but with Tiktok Analytics, you can get a feeling of what works and doesn't and wok accordingly.

8. Plan your Content

It pays to always have a plan when it comes to your content. Just doing thing off the cuff will not cut it one bit. Yes, it's possible to make a video on the fly and have it go viral and you should do this once in while you never know.

But it's always better to have a plan and create a posting schedule and stick it. This is consistency and predictability. And it also helps with performance analysis. So, when you so what works simply rinse and repeat.

Some more:

In-Feed Video Best Practices
Tips for making great TikTok ads

1. Create with Vertical Video in Mind

To maximize user and brand experience, all video assets should look as native as possible and fit the ad specs.

2. Ensure Important Elements of the Video are Centred

TikTok's app interface partially obscures the outer edges of the video frame.

3. Design with a Sound on Environment in Mind

All TikTok videos automatically play with sound on, and no subtitles or captions are required.

4. Keep Videos Short

The video must be under 15 seconds, but we recommend approximately under 10 seconds to retain user attention.

5. Start with a High-Impact Visual

Be aware that users can quickly swipe to the next video unless there's a clear hook for them to keep watching.

6. Write Concise and Informative Captions

Users may not finish watching the entire video, so be sure to include critical information within the caption.

7. Include a Strong Call-to-Action

If you want users to perform a specific action, encourage them to do so clearly and directly in the caption or through the native CTA button.

8. Leverage Influencer Content to Drive Optimal Engagement

Whether or not the influencers are TikTok exclusive, influencer content generally outperforms other asset types—be sure to include them in the first 2 seconds of your video.

CONCLUSION

You have in your hands all that you need to get on Tiktok and market your business. Like I said, you have a better understanding of the platform than millions of businesses across the globe and this is your advantage, so, use it.

With over 500 million users and counting, you are uniquely positioned to benefit as the platform continues to grow its user base.

User on the platform are looking for fun and entertainment and as well as the opportunity to participate in the fun. Brands that get this stands to gain. You need to make sure that your posts and videos reflect this reality.

Again, bear in mind that there are more business getting on-board and if you are not there better get on it. There is power in terms of marketing using the platform. And till the platform gets saturated, this power will continue to grow. So, get in there and cave out a place for your brand.

The ball is now in your court as they say. Just reading this without any actions on your part is as good not buying this book. It does you no good nor your customers. You owe it to them to help them more effectively and efficiently as much as possible and to reach them wherever they may be.

So, download the app and sign up and get to work.

One piece of caution though, like everything else you will do for your business, you need to commit to it. Be sure this is something you have the energy and resources to do and then get on with it and be consistent. It will do you no good to post a bunch of videos and then disappear for weeks on end.

Neither will it be a good thing to posts a lot pictures all the time assuming you have the resources. You need to give users time to take action on your campaign before you post about another one. Just a bit of common sense.

I hope that with this book I have achieved my aim to help inform you on a fast growing and relatively new entrant into the social media scene, Tiktok. Don't put it off anymore but get started as soon as you can marketing on Tiktok. I wish you every success as you apply the strategies you learned in this little book.

BONUS

This is My Way of Saying Thank You. You'll Also Get These Fast Action Bonuses...

Fast Action Bonus #1 – TikTok Marketing - Cheat Sheet (Valued at $27)

This cheat sheet is a handy checklist that makes it easy to get started.

It breaks up the entire guide into easy-to-follow steps so that you can make sure you have all the highlights of everything covered inside right at your fingertips.

Fast Action Bonus #2 – TikTok Marketing - Mind Map (Valued at $17)

Some people learn better by looking at a mind map. The mind map gives you an overview of everything covered inside the guide. You can also print it out for quick reference anytime you need it!

Fast Action Bonus #3 – TikTok Marketing - Resource Guide (Valued at $17)

The Resource Guide gives you a quick point of reference to all of the resources mentioned throughout the guide.

This is my way of saying thank to you for buying this book. To get the bonus, click the link below to download the pdf and enjoy!

DOWNLOAD YOUR FREE PDFs

PLEASE WRITE A REVIEW!

If this book helped you out in anyway, please

help me to help others by writing a review!

CLICK HERE TO LEAVE A REVIEW

Still, if you did not get anything new from this book or you were not impacted in some way, I would still like to hear what you have to say. Either way, I will know what am doing right or wrong and to improve in the future. I wouldn't like to take your money and not deliver. So please, take just 2 minutes to let me know what you think.

Everyone is searching for help on how to improve their lives for the better and one thing they do look for are reviews. If this book has a lot amazing reviews with great comments, they will buy the book and read it and so the ripples effects of goodness spreads. But if it doesn't have any great reviews and comments, they don't buy the book and read it.

I know this book can positively impact and help someone and you can help that person by writing your thoughts and takeaways from the book.

Additionally, I would like to read your review and hear how this book has helped you in anyway at shape or form. My plan is to print every single review and hang them on my home office wall to read for inspiration and motivation throughout the day.

Your great review helps me personally to stay focused and be able to validate all the hard work and lots of hours invested in preparing this book for you.

CLICK THE LINK TO LEAVE A REVIEW

Thank you again for reading this book and all of your support, I am truly honoured and grateful to have been of help. I look forward to helping you make this year the best ever for you and your family!

www.ingramcontent.com/pod-product-compliance
Lightning Source LLC
Chambersburg PA
CBHW070304220526
45465CB00004B/1747